Birds of Prey
Coloring Book

by John Green

Text by Alan Weissman

Dover Publications, Inc., *New York*

Bibliographical Note

Birds of Prey Coloring Book is a new work, first published by
Dover Publications, Inc., in 1989.

International Standard Book Number

ISBN-13: 978-0-486-25989-5
ISBN-10: 0-486-25989-7

Manufactured in the United States by Courier Corporation
25989718   2015
www.doverpublications.com

Introduction

Every day, birds of prey (also called *raptors*) enter into our lives, if only commercially, as with the Bald Eagle in advertisements for the U.S. Postal Service. Of course the symbolic associations of birds of prey go far deeper. For ages, vultures have been associated with death, eagles with power and freedom, hawks with sly thievery and sharp eyesight, falcons with dazzling speed and royal sport, owls with the weird and occult. Most of us have also directly witnessed the majesty of the soaring hawk or eagle, or heard an owl's eerie midnight hooting.

As familiar as these birds are, no one understands exactly what a "bird of prey" is. Songbirds are not thought of as birds of prey, yet there are some, the shrikes, that routinely kill and eat other birds. On the other hand, many vultures, very closely related to the hawks and considered "birds of prey," lack the strong grasping talons of their cousins and take little or no live prey; a number of hawks and owls subsist almost entirely on insects, as do swallows, wrens, and flycatchers; and there are even one or two species of raptors that feed largely on the fruits of palm trees in Africa!

Even the grouping of hawks and owls in the same category, while convenient and traditional, has no solid biological foundation, for a hawk and an owl are no closer kin than either is to a chicken. Hawks (and their allies) and owls belong to two distinct orders of birds: the Falconiformes and the Strigiformes, respectively. Probably the reason for their longtime association is the numerous similarities between many hawks and many owls, such as their sharp, hooked bills, powerful curved claws, and even the habit of regurgitating pellets composed of the bones and other indigestible parts of their prey. And of course many hawks and many owls do kill and eat mammals and birds. These similarities are attributable to the biological phenomenon of "convergent evolution," the same principle that accounts for the existence of bats and whales—mammals that fly like birds and swim like fish. Tradition, as well as the prevalence of similarities attributable to convergent evolution, justifies our keeping the hawks and owls together in this coloring book.

All members of both orders of birds are capable fliers. Some, like many eagles and vultures, are known for spectacular soaring ability. Others, like the Peregrine Falcon, are among the fastest and most agile birds in the world. While owls cannot rival most falconiform birds in speed and soaring ability, many are the world's *quietest* predatory birds, their wings muffled with downy feathers to facilitate silent attacks on unwary prey in the dark.

Hawks and their allies are almost exclusively *diurnal* (active by day), while owls are principally, though far from exclusively, *nocturnal* (active by night). All birds of both orders are equipped with excellent vision. A hawk soaring over a meadow can spot a mouse moving in the grass hundreds of feet below. The vision of owls has a notable peculiarity: owls cannot move their eyes in their sockets. In compensation, however, they can turn their heads all the way around. Contrary to popular belief, even nocturnal owls can see perfectly well in the daytime; in addition, they have highly developed night vision. And some owls are equipped as well with an extraordinary sense of hearing, which enables them to detect the precise location of a faint sound in total darkness. A few birds of prey also have a highly developed sense of smell. It is now believed that the Turkey Vulture combines its sense of smell with keen vision to locate the dead animals it feeds on.

The nesting habits of birds of prey are extremely varied. Most falcons, owls, and New World vultures do not build their own nest, laying their eggs on a bare ledge or, for example, in an old woodpecker hole or an abandoned nest of another type of bird. Most other birds of prey build their own nest, sometimes a bulky, elaborate structure. The eggs of owls are as a rule more perfectly rounded than those of other birds.

The size of birds of prey varies greatly. The Andean Condor can reach four feet long with an impressive wingspan of ten feet. At the other extreme, some falcons and owls are no bigger than sparrows.

Many questions remain to be answered about these fascinating birds. A little of what we do know is given in the captions to the drawings that follow. These represent 42 species, about ten percent of the world's total, which includes about 275 species of hawks and their allies, and 135 of owls. In the descriptions of coloration, there is no room to convey more than a general impression; further details may be seen in the color versions of the drawings, on the inside and outside covers. The drawings are presented in taxonomic order (based on considerations of anatomy and evolution), as given in *Birds of Prey of the World*, by Mary Louise Grossman and John Hamlet (Bonanza Books, New York, 1964). As there is much disagreement among ornithologists regarding the precise taxonomy of hawks and owls, this arrangement must not be considered final. The forms of the birds' names follow more recent sources. Alphabetical lists of both common and scientific names of the birds depicted will be found on page 48.

Andean Condor (*Vultur gryphus*). COLORATION: Black, gray, and white, with pinkish head. Males have a fleshy growth on the forehead called a *caruncle*. This enormous vulture (four feet long) of western and southern South America may soar for hours high in the Andes Mountains on wings spread up to ten feet. It frequents open country, including the seashore, feeding mostly on dead mammals and fish. The Andean Condor breeds only every other year, nesting on ledges or in crevices at over ten thousand feet in altitude. Young birds take about six years to mature, but the total lifespan can be very long, up to 65 years in captive birds.

Turkey Vulture (*Cathartes aura*). COLORATION: Dark brown with red head (gray in immature birds). Popularly called "buzzard" in the United States, the Turkey Vulture, ranging from central Alberta to Tierra del Fuego, is the commonest and most widespread of the New World vultures (a different family from those of the Old World).

A large bird (up to about 29 inches long), it soars patiently for hours on massive, slightly uptilted wings until it spots or smells a dead animal. Soon after one bird descends to feed, all the vultures for miles around swoop in to join it.

5

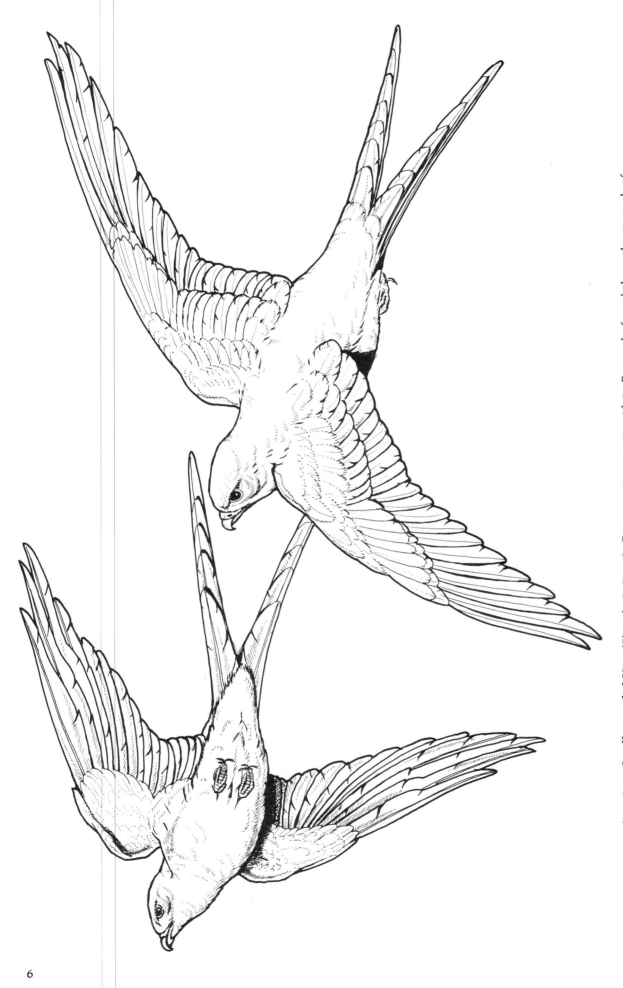

American Swallow-tailed Kite (*Elanoides forficatus*). COL-ORATION: Black and white. Although closely related to various other hawks, the kites form a distinct subgroup of their own. The American Swallow-tailed Kite is a particularly fast, graceful flier, suddenly descending upon a small snake or lizard, or catching and devouring insects in midair. Formerly found throughout much of the central and eastern United States, this medium-sized raptor (about 21 inches to the tip of its long, forked tail) is now restricted to the extreme southeastern United States, as well as parts of tropical Central and South America (including Mexico).

Snail Kite (*Rostrhamus sociabilis*). COLORATION: Males are slaty black with black-and-white tail and orange-red face. On females, the black is replaced by dark brown and there are white patches around the bill. One of the most unusual raptors, this kite is a specialist, feeding only on a certain large marsh snail, which it pries out of the shell with its thin, specially curved bill. About 16 inches long, the Snail Kite is found widely throughout tropical and subtropical America. Loss of suitable snail-breeding habitat has severely reduced and restricted the populations of south Florida (where it was formerly called the Everglade Kite).

Red Kite (*Milvus milvus*). COLORATION: Streaked whitish head and brown back, black primaries (main flight feathers), and bright cinnamon tail. This large kite (24 inches long) of Europe, Asia Minor, and North Africa displays the nimble, buoyant flight of kites but also soars like a Buteo (see pages 11–15, below). Like many kites, it shares with the vultures the habit of eating carrion. It will also eat almost anything else it can catch and kill, from frogs to chickens to mice.

8

Northern Goshawk (*Accipiter gentilis*). COLORATION: Gray and white. This bird and the Sharp-shinned Hawk (next page) represent the Accipiters, a large group of principally forest-dwelling hawks with short, broad wings and long tails, which enable them to maneuver skillfully through dense forest in pursuit of their favorite prey, birds. The Northern Goshawk, a large, pugnacious raptor of worldwide distribution, 20–24 inches long, also consumes many mammals, including rabbits and squirrels. The bird shown here is a trained hawk, fitted with *jesses* (straps of leather on its legs) and bells. Though not falcons, Goshawks have sometimes been used in the ancient sport of falconry.

Sharp-shinned Hawk (*Accipiter striatus*). COLORATION: Dark slate gray, with rusty-barred underparts. Immature birds are brown, with white, brown-streaked underparts. This small American Accipiter (10–14 inches long), like its Old World counterpart the Eurasian Sparrowhawk, feeds almost exclusively on small birds, which it chases down or approaches stealthily, seizes, and then squeezes to death with its powerful talons. As with many birds of prey, particularly bird hawks, the female Sharp-shinned Hawk is considerably larger than the male. Unlike Buteos, Accipiters do not often soar, but, typically, alternately flap their wings a few times and glide.

Red-tailed Hawk (*Buteo jamaicensis*). COLORATION: Brown and white, with rusty tail (plumage highly variable, partly depending upon geographical race). Along with the next four species, the Red-tailed Hawk belongs to the large group called Buteos (or buzzards in England, not to be confused with the vultures, or "buzzards," of the New World). With their practice of circling high in the sky on motionless wings, Buteos are among the hawks most commonly recognized as hawks by most people. The fairly sizable (19–22 inches long) Red-tailed Hawk is common throughout most of North and Central America, including the Caribbean. It will take almost any animal food on occasion but favors rodents, particularly mice.

11

Swainson's Hawk (*Buteo swainsoni*). COLORATION: Brown and white (highly variable). This hawk is slightly smaller (17–21 inches long) than the Red-tailed Hawk and has wings somewhat slenderer. A common Buteo of open country in western North America, Swainson's Hawk feeds mostly on rodents, insects, reptiles, and amphib-ians. Like many Buteos (the eastern American Broad-winged Hawk, for example), Swainson's Hawk is noted for its spectacular migrations; in the late summer, birds amass by the hundreds and slowly wend their way southward. Most spend the winter in Argentina.

Ferruginous Hawk (*Buteo regalis*). COLORATION: Black, white, and rusty. The Ferruginous Hawk is a large (23–25 inches long) Buteo of the plains and prairies of the western United States and Canada. Like the similar Northern Rough-legged Hawk, the Ferruginous Hawk frequently hovers over one spot while hunting. Or it may wait patiently on the ground for a prairie dog or ground squirrel to leave its burrow. It also preys heavily on a variety of other rodents, as well as jackrabbits, and will occasionally take reptiles, birds, and insects. Ordinarily a peaceful neighbor, the Ferruginous Hawk will attack even a Great Horned Owl if its nest is threatened.

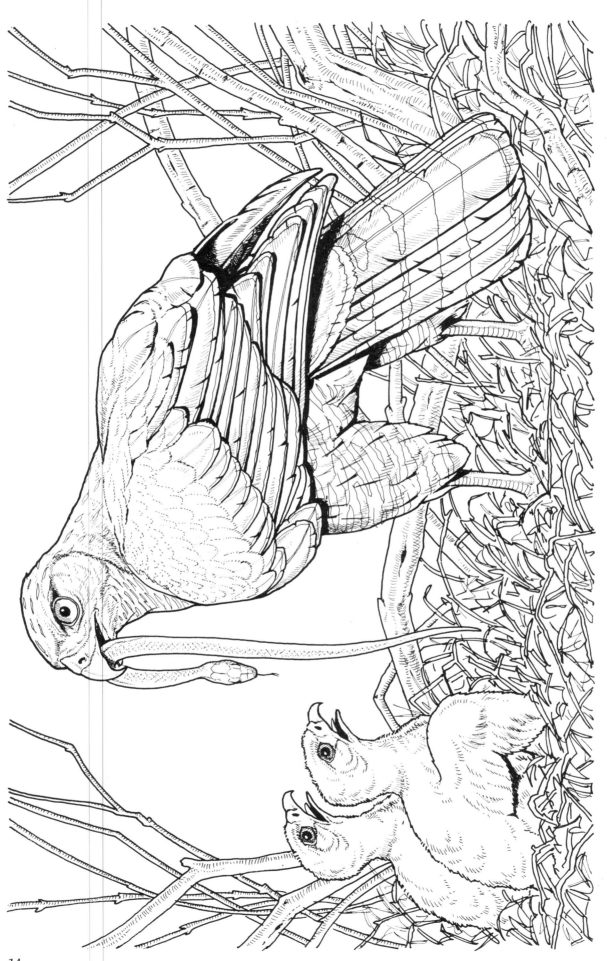

Gray Hawk (*Buteo nitidus*). COLORATION: Gray, with black and white. This medium-sized (15–17 inches long) Buteo of the American tropics and subtropics is found in the United States only in parts of Arizona, New Mexico, and Texas. Its flight resembles that of an Accipiter rather than a typical Buteo. It feeds largely on snakes, lizards, other reptiles, and amphibians.

Common Black-Hawk (*Buteogallus anthracinus*). COLORA-TION: Black, with white on the tail. The medium-sized (18–21 inches long) Common Black-Hawk is far from common in the United States, a few breeding in southern Arizona and Texas; it is, however, common from Mexico through northern South America. Most of the year this is a relatively sluggish hawk, but at nesting time it engages in spectacular displays of aerial prowess. Its diet is somewhat atypical for a Buteo, since it takes fish as well as lizards, frogs, insects, and, in some areas, large quantities of crabs.

Harpy Eagle (*Harpia harpyja*). COLORATION: Black, gray, and white. Eagles, like most raptors, tend to fall into groups of birds with similar appearance and habits. The monstrous Harpy Eagle (over three feet long) is a rarely seen denizen of tropical American rainforests. Armed with heavy, powerful feet, it feeds on monkeys (like the similar Philippine Monkey-eating Eagle and African Crowned Eagle), as well as sloths, other mammals, and some birds.

Long-crested Hawk Eagle (*Lophoaetus occipitalis*). COLORATION: Dark brown or black, with areas of white. As fierce-looking as its similarly crested relatives, the Long-crested Hawk Eagle is actually a smaller, tamer eagle, about 19–22 inches long, of open forests and savannas of sub-Saharan Africa. It preys upon rodents and various other small vertebrates and invertebrates, sometimes picking off mice fleeing from grass fires.

17

Golden Eagle (*Aquila chrysaetos*). COLORATION: Brown, with an amber-brown tinge on the head and neck. The eagles of the genus *Aquila* form a distinct group, generally inhabiting remote, mountainous country. The Golden Eagle is a huge, powerful eagle, 30–40 inches long, found widely throughout the Northern Hemisphere. Generally Golden Eagles are content to feed on small mammals, such as hares and ground squirrels, but, when faced with starvation in the far north, these birds, hunting in twos and threes, have been known to bring down full-grown deer and pronghorn antelopes. They are capable of surprisingly swift flight.

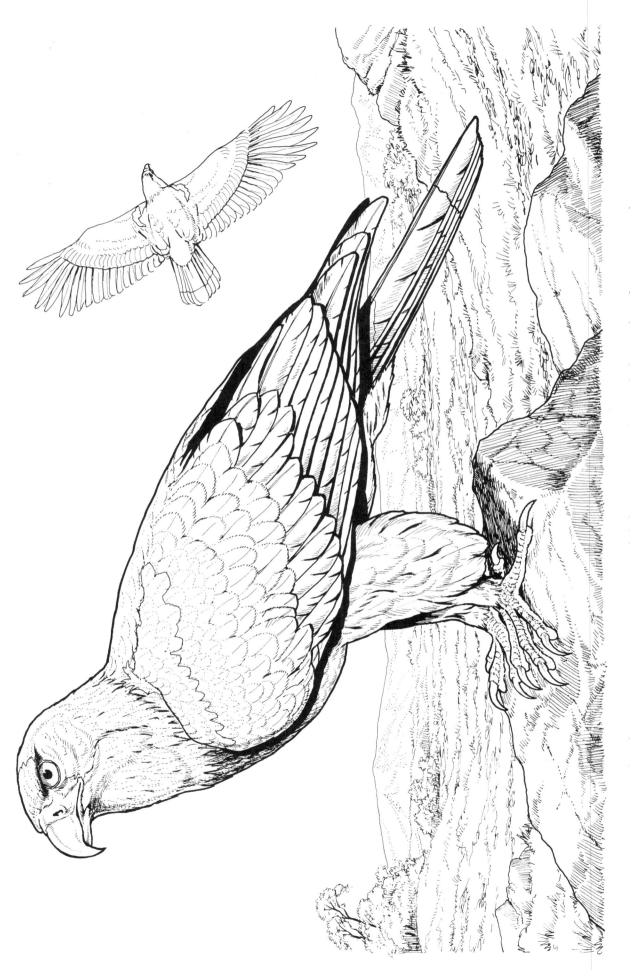

Imperial Eagle (*Aquila heliaca*). COLORATION: Dark, light, and medium brown, with white shoulder patches. The Imperial Eagle is a slightly smaller (up to 35 inches long) cousin of the Golden Eagle, found in western and central Asia and parts of Africa and southern Europe. Like many eagles, it builds an enormous nest high in an isolated tree and hunts in nearby open country, generally preying upon small mammals.

19

Bald Eagle (*Haliaeetus leucocephalus*). COLORATION: Dark brown, with white head and tail. As an official emblem of the United States, the Bald Eagle is familiar to many who have never seen the live bird. The only eagle restricted to North America, it is, however, closely related to a number of other similar fishing eagles (of the group "sea eagles"). An opportunist, the Bald Eagle will steal fish from Ospreys, pick up dead fish from the shore, or catch its own fish or, sometimes, ducks or small mammals. The distinctive white head and tail do not appear until the bird is about four years old. (Size: 31–37 inches long.)

White-tailed Eagle (*Haliaeetus albicilla*). COLORATION: Brown, with white tail. The White-tailed Eagle is the Eurasian counterpart of the Bald Eagle: it is almost the same size (26–35 inches long), is found in similar habitat, and eats the same kind of food. Both birds also build the same kind of nest, a massive stick nest, usually high in a tree or on a cliff, to which the birds return year after year. This sea eagle is also found in parts of Greenland and Iceland.

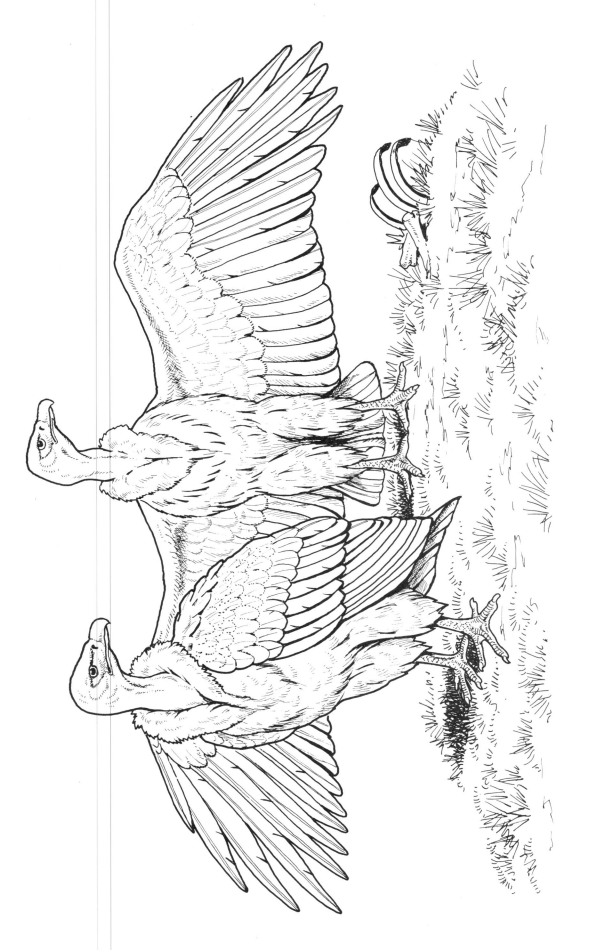

Griffon Vulture (*Gyps fulvus*). COLORATION: Olive, tan, brown, and black body, with white head and ruff. Not closely related to the New World (Cathartid) vultures, the Old World (Accipitrine) vultures are, rather, close kin to the more typical hawks and eagles. The Griffon Vulture (over 40 inches long) is found in parts of southern Europe, Asia, and Africa. Where many species of vultures coexist, they usually specialize in different parts of an animal carcass. When a more powerful vulture has ripped open an animal's hide, the Griffon Vultures, with their grotesquely long necks, can come in to feed on the inner organs.

Egyptian Vulture (*Neophron percnopterus*). COLORATION: Mostly white, with brown and black; yellow face patch. The relatively small Egyptian Vulture (22–25 inches long) is found in most of Africa, except rain forests, and in southern Europe and Southeast Asia. It is at the bottom of the vulturine feeding chain, joining crows and other small scavengers in eating scraps left by the larger carrion-feeding birds. An undiscriminating feeder, the Egyptian Vulture will search garbage heaps for anything digestible, may take live mice and crabs, and has even been known to feed on dates.
(Note: Birds of the order Falconiformes continue on page 26.)

Common Barn-Owl (*Tyto alba*). COLORATION: Tawny or rusty and white, with light spots. This strange-looking bird, about 16 inches long, is found on six continents in tropic and temperate zones, yet even where most common it is rarely seen, for it is strictly nocturnal. While most owls belong to the family Typical Owls, a relatively few, including the Common Barn-Owl, belong to a separate family, Barn Owls (some ornithologists have established a third small family, Bay Owls). Common Barn-Owls nest in corners of old barns (hence their name), holes in trees, and other natural and artificial structures, including man-made nest boxes. These owls

do not hoot but make various weird screeching, rasping, and clicking sounds, which have frightened many a solitary midnight traveler in the country, though Barn-Owls are harmless to man. Mice have more reason to fear Barn-Owls, since their excellent night vision, specially designed hearing, silent flight, and powerful talons make them extraordinarily efficient mousers. In addition to large quantities of mice and other small rodents, Barn-Owls have been known to eat other small animals, birds, and even insects.

(As the center spread, the drawing of this bird is out of its taxonomic place. Owls continue on page 38.)

Lammergeier (*Gypaetus barbatus*). COLORATION: Buff, with brown wings; white face has patches of black bristles. The Lammergeier, or Bearded Vulture, is a very large (over 40 inches long, with 10-foot wingspread) and very unusual vulture with a food specialty of its own: bones, the larger of which it smashes by dropping them on rocks. It also eats carrion as well as some live prey. The Lammergeier inhabits high plains and mountains of the Old World, in Spain, Sicily, Sardinia, East Africa, and western and central Asia, including the Himalayas at altitudes of over 25,000 feet.

Northern Harrier (*Circus cyaneus*). COLORATION: Male: blue-gray and white; black wingtips. Female: brown and white, streaked. Immature birds (both sexes) resemble females but have rich cinnamon underparts. The "harriers" form a distinct group of hawks (actually a subfamily), typically soaring leisurely low over the ground in search of reptiles, frogs, birds, insects, and, especially, rodents. The widespread Northern Harrier (17–23 inches long), or Hen Harrier, as it is called in Europe (also Marsh Hawk in North America), is found in much of the Northern Hemisphere. Harriers have a slight facial "disk" like owls, which apparently helps them locate prey by hearing.

27

African Harrier Hawk (*Gymnogenys typicus*). COLORATION: Dove gray with black-and-white barring, white on tail, and yellow face patch. The African Harrier Hawk (about 20 inches long) is found in most of sub-Saharan Africa, especially savannas. This somewhat atypical harrier courses over the ground but also probes hollows of trees for such food as lizards and termites. In some areas it feeds on palm nuts, in others on the eggs and young of Weaver Birds.

Bateleur (*Terathopius ecaudatus*). COLORATION: Black, gray, and tan; red-orange facial patch. Females have gray wing secondaries (males black). The Bateleur (French for "tumbler," after its acrobatic flying habits) of Africa is a middle-sized (22–25 inches long) raptor of the Old World group "serpent eagles." Appropriately, snakes are a favorite food. This long-winged, short-tailed bird of the air (it may swoop about for hours without alighting) will also eat many other kinds of food, from birds' eggs and grasshoppers to rats and carrion. It is also a pirate, harassing and robbing other birds.

Osprey (*Pandion haliaetus*). COLORATION: Brown and white, with black patches. Female shows more distinct streaking on chest. The Osprey is a medium-sized raptor, 21–23 inches long, found near water throughout much of the world. Belonging to a subfamily of its own (some ornithologists say a separate family), the Osprey feeds almost exclusively on fish. Typically it soars over water until it spots a fish, then plunges dramatically into the water and grabs its prey with feet bearing rough scales and reversible outer toes to facilitate grasping. The Osprey then brings its catch to a favorite perch and consumes it a small piece at a time.

Crested Caracara (*Polyborus plancus*). COLORATION: Brown and white; red-orange facial patch. The Crested Caracara is one of the world's strangest birds. Taxonomically related to the falcons, it often feeds on carrion with the vultures. But it will eat almost anything, dead or alive, from worms to rabbits. This 22-inch-long raptor is the only caracara (a New World group) found north of Mexico, ranging from Tierra del Fuego to Arizona, Texas, and Florida. Unlike most falcons, it builds a large stick nest, and it frequently runs on the ground with its unusually long legs.

Gyrfalcon (*Falco rusticolus*). COLORATION: Highly variable, from dark gray-brown through white. Falcons are a large, well-known group of raptors that form a separate family (including the caracaras). Typically they are sleek, trim birds with long, pointed wings and a notch on the bill used to sever the spinal cord of prey. Their flight is normally very fast. Many species are very widely distributed. The Gyrfalcon, the largest (20–25 inches long) and most powerful, is found all across the Northern Hemisphere, mainly in the far north. It takes such prey as ptarmigan, ducks, and lemmings.

Prairie Falcon (*Falco mexicanus*). COLORATION: Pale brown, with black and white. The Prairie Falcon is a medium-sized falcon (16–19 inches long) of the dry, open country of western North America. The food of this raptor varies. It may stoop at (dive upon) a flying grouse and, reaching enormous speed, knock the bird, as large as itself, out of the air. Or, with far less dignity, the Prairie Falcon may decide to hop about on the ground and pick up grasshoppers. Mammals as large as jackrabbits are also eaten.

Peregrine Falcon (*Falco peregrinus*). COLORATION: Regionally variable; typically dark gray with black head and light, streaked underparts. The noble Peregrine Falcon (15–20 inches long) is the bird that has been most frequently used in the ancient sport of falconry. The Peregrine, an extremely graceful, nimble, acrobatic flier, will fly high and then stoop at a bird at lightning speed (estimated at up to, or even exceeding, 200 miles an hour), often knocking its prey clear out of the sky. It will then follow its victim to the ground, seize it, and with its notched bill immediately sever the spinal cord at the neck, in the manner of all falcons, often entirely decapi-

tating small birds. The bird is then plucked before being eaten (often only a few choice portions are consumed). Most of the food of Peregrine Falcons consists of birds, from sparrows to sandpipers to ducks, but occasionally a small mammal is taken. They have been known to nest on bridges and skyscrapers in cities and feed on the plentiful supply of pigeons. Now recovering from a decline in population due to pesticide poisoning, the Peregrine Falcon is found almost everywhere in suitable habitat. Formerly called Duck Hawk in the United States.

Merlin (*Falco columbarius*). COLORATION: Variable. Females generally have brown upperparts, males gray. Both have streaked underparts and black-and-white striped tails. The Merlin shares many of the habits of its larger cousins (it is about 10–13 inches long) but does not generally stoop at its prey. Its food consists principally of small birds, taken by sudden bursts of speed in direct flight. A Merlin will persistently dash into a flock of pigeons (it was once called the Pigeon Hawk in the United States) until it catches one. The Merlin is found around the world in the Northern Hemisphere.

American Kestrel (*Falco sparverius*). COLORATION: Rusty, gray, black, and white. Males have blue-gray on wings. Kestrels form a subgroup among falcons. They typically hover over one spot, then swoop down to take prey on the ground. Their food, more varied than that of typical falcons, includes insects, reptiles, amphibians, mice, and small birds. The American Kestrel (formerly called the Sparrow Hawk) is the smallest, as well as the commonest, falcon in the United States (9–11 inches long) but is also found throughout most of the Western Hemisphere.

(Note: Owls [Strigiformes] begin on page 24.)

Eastern Screech-Owl (*Otus asio*). COLORATION: Two types, or "phases": reddish, with black and white; and gray, with brown, black, and white. This small owl (8–9 inches long) is widespread in eastern North America, though not quite so widespread since the European Starling began competing with it for nesting sites (both nest in holes in trees). Screech-Owls favor rodents and small birds but will eat almost anything, from spiders to fish to snails, even swallowing flying insects on the wing in the manner of Whip-poor-wills. These secretive, nocturnal owls are expert at camouflaging themselves as woody stubs on branches of trees in the daytime.

Great Horned Owl (*Bubo virginianus*). COLORATION: Mottled and barred brown and orange, with black and white. This large, powerful owl (18–25 inches long) is widespread in the Western Hemisphere. A truly formidable predator, the Great Horned Owl typically preys upon rabbits, rats, pheasants, and squirrels, but may take even turkeys, snakes, hawks, other owls, foxes, skunks, and porcupines. The owls seem not to mind the odor of the skunks but do not always emerge victorious from conflicts with the sharp-quilled porcupines. Sometimes active by day.

Snowy Owl (*Nyctea scandiaca*). COLORATION: Primarily white, with black. Males whiter than females. This large (20–24 inches long), fierce predator of the far north (in both Old and New Worlds) nests on mounds on open tundra north of the tree line. When their prey, generally ptarmigan, lemmings, and various other birds, mam-mals, and sometimes fish, becomes scarce owing to harsh winters or population "crashes," Snowy Owls "invade" areas far south of their usual winter range. At rare intervals they have turned up in such unlikely places as Yugoslavia and Louisiana.

Elf Owl (*Micrathene whitneyi*). COLORATION: Various shades of brown, with black and white. The tiny Elf Owl, under 6 inches long—scarcely larger than most wrens—makes its home in old woodpecker holes in trees and the saguaro cactus of the southwest United States and parts of Mexico. Where nesting holes are scarce it has been known to share saguaro holes with families of woodpeckers and other birds. Common in much of their range, Elf Owls are rarely seen because of their nocturnal habits. Most of their food consists of various insects.

Burrowing Owl (*Athene cunicularia*). COLORATION: Chocolate brown and white. This long-legged owl is a ground dweller of grasslands from southern South America through western North America, as well as parts of Florida and the Caribbean. About 9 inches long (up to 12 inches in higher-altitude populations), Burrowing Owls occupy holes dug by prairie dogs, skunks, armadillos, and other ground-dwelling animals. Their food, sometimes taken in the daytime, consists mostly of insects but also of almost any small vertebrates or invertebrates available. When threatened in its burrow, the Burrowing Owl can effectively imitate the sound of a rattlesnake.

African Wood Owl (*Ciccaba woodfordii*). COLORATION: Chocolate brown, with white. The African Wood Owl is a medium-sized (12–14 inches long) owl found in densely wooded areas throughout much of western, central, and southern Africa; it is particularly common in some regions where mice are plentiful. It also consumes a variety of insects, rodents, reptiles, and small birds. Several similar species of Wood Owls inhabit the forests of tropical America.

Barred Owl (*Strix varia*). COLORATION: Dark grayish brown, yellow-orange, and white. The Barred Owl, one of a large, worldwide group of *Strix* owls, is found in eastern and central North America and parts of Central America. Known for its ability to fly gracefully through dense woods, as well as for its noisy hooting, this medium-sized owl (14–18 inches long, variable regionally) seems to prefer a diet of mice but, like many other owls, will eat almost any small mammal, bird, reptile, amphibian, fish, or insect available.

Great Gray Owl (*Strix nebulosa*). COLORATION: Streaked gray with brown. The huge size (up to 30 inches long) of this denizen of northern woods is deceptive, for under a mass of feathers is a bird much less robust than the Great Horned Owl. Frequently active by day, the Great Gray Owl is found chiefly in dense coniferous and mixed boreal forests in Canada, parts of the northern United States, and Norway through Siberia in the Old World. When its prey, consisting mostly of rabbits and other small mammals, becomes scarce, it may wander somewhat south of its usual range, though not to the extent of the Snowy Owl.

Short-eared Owl (*Asio flammeus*). COLORATION: Dark brown and tawny, streaked, with black and white. The Short-eared Owl is named for its two little "ears," actually tufts of feathers, invisible at any distance. This middle-sized owl (about 15 inches long) is a bird of very broad distribution, thriving in places as far removed as Baffin Island, Hawaii, and Finland. Short-eared Owls differ in their habits from even closely related birds. Frequently abroad by day, they fly low over meadows, like harriers, searching for rodents. They tend to congregate in areas overpopulated by mice, which they are particularly efficient at catching.

Northern Saw-whet Owl (*Aegolius acadicus*). COLORA-TION: Streaked brown, reddish-brown, and white. This little owl (7–8 inches long), strictly nocturnal and secretive, is rarely seen even where most common. When one is discovered in its daytime roost, often in the dense foliage of a conifer, it is extremely tame, frequently allowing itself to be held in the hand. Feeding chiefly on mice, the Northern Saw-whet Owl is found in most of North America, including parts of Mexico, except in the extreme south-central and southeastern United States. Its "saw-whet" call—one among many—has reminded some of the sound of a grasshopper.

Alphabetical List of Scientific Names

Alphabetical List of Common Names